Liberal Democrat
Manifesto 2010

D1585954

table of contents

We've had 65 years of Labour and the Conservatives: the same parties taking turns and making the same mistakes, letting you down. It is time for something different. It is time for something better.

Dear Friend,

Elections that can really make a difference don't come along very often. But this is one of them.

This May, you have an opportunity to shape the future of our country for the better. We've had 65 years of Labour and the Conservatives: the same parties taking turns and making the same mistakes, letting you down. They have taught people to expect little from politics, and get less.

It is time for something different. It is time for something better.

Doesn't it make you angry that after 65 years of red-blue government, a child's chances in life are still more determined by their parents' bank balance than by their own hopes and dreams? Doesn't it make you angry that the banks have been allowed to ride roughshod over our economy, and are still handing out bonuses by the bucket load? That politics is still the plaything of wealthy donors and corrupt MPs? That despite endless warm words from politicians, our climate is in danger? That the poorest are the ones who pay the biggest chunk of their income in tax?

I was brought up to believe that the way things are is not the way they have to be. I was brought up to believe that you should fight for what you believe in, and fight for change. So my message for you in this election is simple.

Don't settle for low politics and broken promises: be more demanding. Set your sights on the Britain you want for your children and your grandchildren, and use your vote to make it happen.

Liberal Democrats are different. When it's come to the big decisions – on the banks, on the environment, on the war in Iraq – we are the only party that has called it right, every time.

Only Liberal Democrats have the big ideas for fundamental, structural changes in the way our country works to make it fair. Only Liberal Democrats will shake up the tax system to put £700 back in the pockets of tens of millions of low and middle-income families, paid for by ensuring the wealthy pay their fair share. Only Liberal Democrats will break up the banks and start Britain building things again, creating a sustainable economy that no longer threatens our planet's future. Only Liberal Democrats will invest in our schools to give every child, no matter their background, a fair start in life. And only Liberal Democrats will sort out our rotten political system once and for all.

A strong vote for the Liberal Democrats means the end of red-blue, blue-red politics. It means the end of the stitch-up between the two old parties. It means the beginning of real change that works for you.

Best wishes,

Nick Clegg

our first priorities:
4 steps to a fairer Britain

fair taxes
that put money back in your pocket

- The first £10,000 you earn tax-free: a tax cut of £700 for most people
- 3.6 million low earners and pensioners freed from income tax completely
- Paid for in full by closing loopholes that unfairly benefit the wealthy and polluters

a fair chance
for every child

- Ensure children get the individual attention they need by cutting class sizes
- Made possible by investing £2.5 billion in schools targeted to help struggling pupils
- Give schools the freedom to make the right choices for their pupils

a fair future
creating jobs by making Britain greener

- Break up the banks and get them lending again to protect real businesses
- Honesty about the tough choices needed to cut the deficit
- Green growth and jobs that last by investing in infrastructure

a fair deal
by cleaning up politics

- Put trust back into politics by giving you the right to sack corrupt MPs
- Restore and protect hard-won British civil liberties with a Freedom Bill
- Overhaul Westminster completely: fair votes, an elected House of Lords, all politicians to pay full British taxes

introduction: our values

This election can be and must be a turning point for Britain. This must be a moment of great change, so that we emerge from the recession as a fairer, greener, stronger and more united society. To do that, we need to be clear and honest about the failures that caused the problems we face, and set a clear, hopeful course for a different, better future.

Britain is struggling to emerge from a long and difficult recession. Families are finding it hard to make ends meet. Millions are unemployed, and millions more have taken pay cuts or reduced hours to stay in their jobs. And there are deeper problems too. Britain, for all its many strengths, is still too unequal and unfair, a country where the circumstances of your birth and the income of your parents still profoundly affect your chances in life. Our children's future is threatened by climate change, which we have done far too little to stop. And the political system is in crisis.

Britain needs a fresh start. We need hope for a different, better future.

That is what this manifesto is all about. We believe that the future must be built on a different foundation: fairness. We believe that there are systemic failures that underlie every one of the major problems we face. And that gives us the chance to reshape our country, fundamentally, for the better.

Fairness is an essential British value. It is at the centre of how the vast majority of British people live their lives, but it has been forgotten by those at the top. Instead, greed and self-interest have held sway over the government and parts of the economy in recent decades. They have forgotten that growth must be shared and sustainable if it is to last.

Our core aim is to hard-wire fairness back into national life. That way we can build a stronger society with growth that lasts, fairness and opportunity for all.

bringing back fairness

At the root of Britain's problems today is the failure to distribute power fairly between people. Political power has been hoarded by politicians and civil servants; economic power has been hoarded by big businesses. Both kinds of power have been stripped from ordinary citizens, leaving us with a fragile society marked by inequality, environmental degradation and boom-bust economics. If government merely tinkers at the edges – the Labour and Conservative approach – Britain's problems will not be solved. We can change this only with radical action.

The Liberal Democrat philosophy is built on a simple ambition: to distribute power fairly among people. From that goal of fairness spring the four priorities which form the backbone of this manifesto. Each will redistribute power of a different kind, be it economic, social, political or financial. **Each will change Britain for the better.**

Those four changes are spelt out in detail in this manifesto. They will make Britain the fair country people want it to be. They are:

- Fair taxes that put money back in your pocket.

- A fair chance for every child.

- A fair future, creating jobs by making Britain greener.

- A fair deal for you from politicians.

our tax plan

We propose the most radical tax reform in a generation, cutting taxes for millions paid for by closing loopholes at the top and increasing taxes on polluting aviation. No tax system should try to create total equality of income – but it can and should help redistribute wealth and power, to alleviate the worst excesses of inequality.

our schools plan

We will give every child the fair start they deserve by providing cash to reduce class sizes and increase one-to-one tuition. This is the best way to ensure, over the long term, that every child has opportunities, no matter their background, their home town or their parents' bank balance.

our economic plan

Our vision is of a very different economy, balanced and sustainable both financially and environmentally. We will reduce the deficit, break up the banks, and ensure that Britain leads in developing the new green economy that the world needs.

our plan for cleaning up politics

The final change is the one that makes the others possible: political reform. The current system exists to block change. We will stamp out corruption and abuse by giving people power to sack corrupt MPs, end big money politics, and make sure those who seek to sit in Parliament pay full UK taxes. We will reinvigorate our democracy by dispersing power, breaking open Westminster and Whitehall and embracing fair votes for every level of election.

These four changes will transform Britain. They are our core priorities. The stronger we are as a party, the more power and influence we will have to make them happen, to change our country for the better. They are all essential to delivering real change in Britain.

This manifesto is not limited to these four structural changes. It is a full programme for a Liberal Democrat government, setting out our approach to all public services, to fiscal discipline, and to Britain's place in the changing world.

In formulating our policies we have been driven by our one abiding concern: fairness. We know these are difficult times. But we also know there is a way out, a way to build a fairer, greener and stronger future.

It will take courage and commitment to make Britain truly fair for our children, and for the future. It will take an extraordinary government, different from every one that has come before. That is what the Liberal Democrats offer, which no other party can at this election.

If you want real change, choose the Liberal Democrats.

a green future: protecting the planet

Liberal Democrats believe that protecting the environment is one of the greatest challenges this generation faces. We must hand on to our children a planet worth living on. That requires action across government – this is everybody's responsibility, not just one climate change minister's. It is because we believe concern for the environment is important in every part of people's lives that we have identified policies in every chapter of this manifesto to protect the planet. These policies are highlighted with green side tabs.

your money. Liberal Democrats want to make the tax and benefits system fair, so that everyone, be they young or old, can afford to get by.

change that works **for you**
BUILDING A FAIRER BRITAIN

fair taxes and fair benefits to help every family get by

Liberal Democrats want to make the tax and benefits system fair, so that everyone, be they young or old, can afford to get by. We have plans for the most radical, far-reaching tax reforms in a generation.

These changes are desperately needed. Conservative and Labour governments have changed Britain into one of the most unequal societies in the developed world, where ordinary people struggle to make ends meet while the richest benefit from tax breaks. The poorest fifth of the population pay a higher proportion of their income in tax than the richest fifth.

We set out in this manifesto a clear plan to **bring the budget back under control**, being honest about the tough choices we need to take. We will **cut taxes for millions of working people and pensioners**, paid for by making sure that the very wealthy pay their fair share and that polluting air travel is properly taxed. We will boost the state pension **by immediately restoring the link with earnings** growth.

tax fairness for everyone

Under a Liberal Democrat government, you will not have to pay any income tax on the first £10,000 you earn. This will put £700 back into the pockets of millions of people on low and middle incomes and free 3.6 million more people on low incomes from having to pay any income tax at all. In this way, we will help people who are struggling to make ends meet and provide an incentive to work and save.

This change will be paid for by:

- Giving tax relief on pensions only at the basic rate, so that everyone gets the same tax relief on their pension contributions.

- Taxing capital gains at the same rates as income, so that all the money you make is taxed in the same way.

- Tackling tax avoidance and evasion, with new powers for HM Revenue & Customs and a law to ensure properties can't avoid stamp duty if they are put into an offshore trust.

- Ensuring pollution is properly taxed by replacing the per-passenger Air Passenger Duty with a per-plane duty (PPD), ensuring that air freight is taxed for the first time. We will also introduce an additional, higher rate of PPD on domestic flights if realistic alternative and less polluting travel is available.

- Introducing a Mansion Tax at a rate of 1 per cent on properties worth over £2 million, paid on the value of the property above that level.

In addition we will reform the system of 'non-domiciled' status, allowing people to hold such status for up to seven years; after that time they will become subject to tax on all offshore income in the same way as domiciled British citizens.

dealing with the deficit

The health of the economy depends on the health of the country's finances. Public borrowing has reached unsustainable levels, and needs to be brought under control to protect the country's economic future.

A Liberal Democrat government will be straight with people about the tough choices ahead. Not only must waste be eliminated, but we must also be bold about finding big areas of spending that can be cut completely. That way we can control borrowing, protect the services people rely on most and still find some money to invest in building a fair future for everyone.

We have already identified over £15 billion of savings in government spending per year, vastly in excess of the £5 billion per year that we have set aside for additional spending commitments. All our spending commitments will be funded from this pool of identified savings, with all remaining savings used to reduce the deficit.

We must ensure the timing is right. If spending is cut too soon, it would undermine the much-needed recovery and cost jobs. We will base the timing of cuts on an objective assessment of economic conditions, not political dogma. Our working assumption is that the economy will be in a stable enough condition to bear cuts from the beginning of 2011–12.

Through making tough choices, as well as increasing efficiency and reducing bureaucracy across government, our savings will include:

- Setting a £400 pay rise cap for all public sector workers, initially for two years, ensuring that the lowest paid are eligible for the biggest percentage rise.

- Restricting tax credits.

- Ending government payments into Child Trust Funds.

- Introducing a Banking Levy so that banks pay for the financial support they have received, until such time as they can be split up in order to insulate retail banking from investment risks.

- Scrapping ID cards and the next generation of biometric passports.

- Cancelling Eurofighter Tranche 3b.

- Scaling back HomeBuy schemes.

- Reforming prisons, including through reducing the number of short sentences.

- Cutting back burdensome regulation of local authorities.

Further details of our savings, including a number of smaller savings items, can be found in the tables annexed to the chapter on Credible and Responsible Finances on page 96.

In the longer term, as part of a Comprehensive Spending Review (CSR) involving wide consultation, we will seek to identify additional savings which can be used to pay down the deficit further. These will include:

- Saying no to the like-for-like replacement of the Trident nuclear weapons system, which could cost £100 billion. We will hold a full defence review to establish the best alternative for Britain's future security.

- Reforming public sector pensions to ensure that they are sustainable and affordable for the long term, with an independent review to agree a settlement that is fair for all taxpayers as well as for public servants.

- Better government IT procurement, investigating the potential of different approaches such as cloud computing and open-source software.

- A wholesale review of value for money in the public sector based on the findings of the National Audit Office and the House of Commons Public Accounts Committee.

We will establish a Council on Financial Stability, involving representatives of all parties, the Governor of the Bank of England and the Chair of the Financial Services Authority. This group would agree the timeframe and scale of a deficit reduction plan to set the framework (not the detail) for the CSR and seek to promote it externally and domestically. Any agreement would be without prejudice to parties retaining and advocating distinctive views on a wide range of issues (such as fair taxes and spending priorities).

fairness in pensions, savings and benefits

Labour has created a hugely complex and unfair benefits system, and it needs to be reformed. Pensions and savings have been undermined.

We will make pensions and benefits fair and reward savers by:

- Immediately restoring the link between the basic state pension and earnings. We will uprate the state pension annually by whichever is the higher of growth in earnings, growth in prices or 2.5 per cent.

- Increasing the income tax threshold to £10,000.

- Giving people greater flexibility in accessing part of their personal pension fund early, for example to help in times of financial hardship.

- Giving people control over their pension by scrapping the rule that compels you to buy an annuity when you reach age 75.

- Allowing individuals to save through our UK Infrastructure Bank, offering stable long-term returns.

- Meeting the government's obligations towards Equitable Life policyholders who have suffered loss. We will set up a swift, simple, transparent and fair payment scheme.

- Ending the rollercoaster of tax credit overpayments by fixing payments for six months at a time. We will also target payments towards those who need them most.

- Reforming Winter Fuel Payments to extend them to all severely disabled people, paid for by delaying age-related Winter Fuel Payments until people reach 65. We will continue to pay Winter Fuel Payments to all current recipients of Pension Credit.

your job. Liberal Democrats want to build an economy that is based on innovation and sustainability, where the infrastructure the country needs is in place for individuals and businesses to thrive.

change that works **for you**

opportunities for all in a fair, green economy

Liberal Democrats want to build an economy that is based on innovation and sustainability, where the infrastructure the country needs is in place for individuals and businesses to thrive. Our aim is to deliver growth that lasts and is environmentally sustainable.

Decades of Labour and Conservative rule have created an unsustainable economy, preoccupied with the artificial wealth of inflated property prices rather than productive work and invention. They have been obsessed by the 'Square Mile' – the City of London – instead of supporting all 100,000 square miles of Britain.

To boost the economy and **create jobs for those who need them**, we will begin our term of office with a one-year economic stimulus and job creation package. To sustain jobs and growth for the long term, we will set up an **Infrastructure Bank** to direct private finance to essential projects such as new rail services and green energy, building the environmentally sustainable economy that is needed for the long term. And to ensure that the economy is never again destabilised by high-risk financial industries, we will **break up the banks** and build up diverse local and regional sources of business finance.

sustainable finance for business growth

We have all learned an important lesson from the credit crunch and the recession: we cannot build an economy on financial gambling. Radical reform of the financial infrastructure is needed to create and sustain jobs, and move towards a sustainable and balanced economy where businesses in every town, city and region can grow.

That starts with banking reform. Banks must be made to behave responsibly. And we need to support and develop new ways of financing growing businesses, with equity rather than debt, and without relying too heavily on the financial centre of the City of London. More diverse sources of finance will provide the funding needed to develop innovative new products and reverse the decline in the UK's manufacturing base.

In order to put the economy on a new footing, we will:

- Break up the banks, to ensure taxpayers are never again expected to underwrite high-risk banking. We would establish a clear separation between low-risk retail banking and high-risk investment banking, and encourage the development of local and regional banks. We will introduce a Banking Levy, so that banks pay for their tax-payer guarantee, until the break-up is complete.

- Get the banks lending responsibly again. The taxpayers' representatives on the boards of the banks the public own or part-own should insist banks lend to viable businesses on fair terms again.

- Ensure that the bonus system can never again encourage banks to behave in a way that puts the financial system at risk or offers rewards for failure.

- Support the establishment of Local Enterprise Funds and Regional Stock Exchanges. Local Enterprise Funds will help local investors put money into growing businesses in their own part of the country and support the development of new products from research to production. Regional Stock Exchanges will be a route for businesses to access equity without the heavy regulatory requirements of a London listing.

creating jobs that last

The new economy must be very different from the old if it is to be sustainable, not just financially, but environmentally too. If we start now, Britain can lead the new green economy that the world needs. We recognise that strong businesses create and sustain jobs and a Liberal Democrat government will support them in doing so.

Liberal Democrats will begin our term in office with a one-year job creation and green economic stimulus package. We have identified £3.1 billion of public spending that can be used to create 100,000 jobs. This programme will be a first step towards our target for a zero-carbon Britain by 2050.

Our green stimulus plan will create 100,000 jobs. It comprises:

- Investing up to £400 million in refurbishing shipyards in the North of England and Scotland so that they can manufacture offshore wind turbines and other marine renewable energy equipment. As part of this scheme we will write off backdated business rates demands from before April 2008 for businesses in ports.

- Launching an 'Eco Cash-Back' scheme, for one year only, which will give you £400 if you install double glazing, replace an old boiler, or install micro-generation. If you choose micro-generation, you will be able to sell the energy back to the National Grid at a profit, with a more attractive feed-in tariff than under current government plans.

- Setting aside extra money for schools who want to improve the energy efficiency of their buildings. They will pay back the loan over time from energy savings, creating a rolling fund to help insulate every public building.

- Bringing 250,000 empty homes back into use. People who own these homes will get a grant or a cheap loan to renovate them so that they can be used: grants if the home is for social housing, loans for private use.

- Investing £140 million in a bus scrappage scheme that helps bus companies to replace old polluting buses with new, accessible low-carbon ones and creates jobs.

We will also create hundreds of thousands of opportunities for young people affected by the recession. A work placement scheme with up to 800,000 places will ensure that young people have the opportunity to gain skills, qualifications and work experience even if they can't find a job. Young people on the scheme would be paid £55 a week for up to three months. We will also fund 15,000 extra Foundation Degree places, fully meet the up-front costs of adult apprenticeships, and increase the Adult Learning Grant to £45 a week for 18–24 year-olds in Further Education.

To help the transition to a green economy over the longer-term, we will set up a United Kingdom Infrastructure Bank (UKIB) to attract private finance – essential to delivering the much-needed expansion of Britain's transport and energy infrastructure when public finances are tight. The UKIB will:

- Create a new route to provide capital, guarantees and equity to infrastructure projects, using public money to attract upfront private investment.

- Increase the funding available from the private sector by tapping into the funds of institutional investors, namely annuity funds looking for a home in the UK.

- Reduce the cost of long-term funding as compared with the Private Finance Initiative.

- Provide the opportunity for retail investors to save in safe long-term assets.

- Be a stand-alone public entity, independent from government but with a long-term strategic remit. It would have the ability to reject or accept proposals based on whether they are financially viable or within its remit.

- Start with government seed funding which it can use as a capital base to borrow against. This seed funding could be raised from the sell-off of the student loan book or the Tote as the government has already proposed. In addition borrowing could be secured against or raised from government-owned assets such as the Dartford Crossing. We will investigate other ways of raising seed capital such as auctioning airport landing slots and parts of the radio spectrum.

enabling enterprise that benefits Britain

Liberal Democrats believe in the value of entrepreneurship and enterprise, recognising that thriving businesses are vital to create the wealth this country needs. We need to ensure a strong competitive environment by providing a level playing field for all businesses, encouraging a diverse, sustainable economy for the long term.

Liberal Democrats will:

- Reduce the burden of unnecessary red tape by properly assessing the cost and effectiveness of regulations before and after they are introduced, using 'sunset clauses' to ensure the need for a regulation is regularly reviewed, and working towards the principle of 'one in, one out' for new rules.

- Put an end to the so-called 'gold-plating' of EU rules, so that British businesses are not disadvantaged relative to their European competitors.

- Reform business rates, creating a fairer system where rates are based on site values rather than rental values and are the responsibility of local authorities. We will make small company relief automatic and also seek to ensure that the burden is spread more equitably between small and large businesses.

- Reform Regional Development Agencies (RDAs) to focus solely on economic development, removing duplication with other parts of government and allowing substantial budget reductions. We will give responsibility for economic development to local authorities. Where existing RDAs have strong local support, they may continue with refocused economic development objectives. Where they do not, they will be scrapped and their functions taken over by local authorities.

- Ensure that takeover rules serve the UK economy. We will restore a public interest test so that a broader range of factors than just competition can be considered by regulators when takeovers are proposed and we will ensure that the outcome of takeover bids is determined by the long-term shareholder base. We will reintroduce the Operating and Financial Review, dropped in November 2005, to ensure that directors' social and environmental duties will have to be covered in company reporting.

- Support public investment in the roll-out of superfast broadband, targeted first at those areas which are least likely to be provided for by the market.

- Keep the tax regime and allowances that apply to the oil and gas industry under review to secure the maximum long-term benefit to the UK economy of the remaining North Sea reserves.

- Use the substantial purchasing power of government to expand the markets for green products and technologies.

supporting mutuals, co-ops and social enterprises

We believe that mutuals, co-operatives and social enterprises have an important role to play in the creation of a more balanced and mixed economy. Mutuals give people a proper stake in the places they work, spreading wealth through society, and bringing innovative and imaginative business ideas to bear on meeting local needs.

We will:

- Give financial regulators a clear objective of maintaining a diversity of providers in the financial services industry.

- Seek to turn Northern Rock into a building society.

- Give both Royal Mail and post offices a long-term future, by separating Post Office Ltd from the Royal Mail and retaining Post Office Ltd in full public ownership. 49 per cent of Royal Mail will be sold to create funds for investment. The ownership of the other 51 per cent will be divided between an employee trust and the government.

- Encourage community-owned renewable energy schemes where local people benefit from the power produced.

- Pass a new Mutuals, Co-operatives and Social Enterprises Bill to bring the law up to date and give responsibility for mutuals to a specific minister.

creating a dynamic environment for science and innovation

Britain's future depends on a vibrant research base and the ability of innovators to exploit the country's intellectual capital to generate new home-grown high tech industries.

Despite Government rhetoric, overall public funding of science in real terms is no higher than it was two decades ago. Britain's Research and Development spend as a proportion of GDP remains near the bottom of the G8. There is no room for complacency.

In the current economic climate it is not possible to commit to growth in spending, but Liberal Democrats recognise the importance of science investment to the recovery and to the reshaping of the economy, making it less reliant on the City of London and creating new green industries instead. We will:

- Respect the convention that the science budget, once allocated through the Comprehensive Spending Review process, is not used for other purposes.

- Ensure that the decisions on the funding of research projects are made on the basis of peer review not Whitehall interference, while recognising the need for government to identify broad strategic priorities in a transparent manner.

- Ensure that all state-funded research, including clinical trials, is publicly accessible and that the results are published and subject to peer review.

- Reform science funding to ensure that genuinely innovative scientific research is identified and supported, instead of basing funding decisions on narrow impact factors.

We need to safeguard the future of the science and engineering workforce and break the vicious cycle linking fewer University science, engineering and maths applicants to fewer teachers with specialist qualifications. We will:

- Tackle the gender gap at all levels of scientific study and research to help increase the supply of scientists.

It is vital that policy, especially that relating to public health, criminal justice and environmental protection, benefits from being based on the best available evidence. We will:

- Safeguard academic freedom and the independence of scientific advisers by amending the Ministerial Code to prevent government from bullying or mistreating advisers and distorting evidence or statistics.

fair treatment at work for everyone

Liberal Democrats want to build a society where everyone has the opportunity to get on in life. Most businesses do a great job of supporting their employees, but there is more to do to tackle discrimination on the grounds of gender, sexuality, age, race, religion or disability. We want to give employees fair opportunities to make the best use of their talents, and greater control over their working lives and conditions.

Women are still paid less than men. It can be hard to juggle work and family life. People from Black, Asian and Minority Ethnic communities are still more likely to suffer discrimination. And there are far too many barriers to work for people with disabilities.

We will change this by:

- Extending the right to request flexible working to all employees.

- Requiring name-blind job application forms to reduce sex and race discrimination in employment, initially for every company with over 100 employees.

- Introducing fair pay audits for every company with over 100 employees to combat discrimination in pay, for example against women. We will also require all public companies to declare in full all remunerations of £200,000 per year or more.

- Giving disabled job seekers better practical help to get to work, using voluntary and private sector providers, as well as JobCentre Plus services. We will also reform Access to Work, so disabled people can apply for jobs with funding already in place for equipment and adaptation that they need.

Our policies on secure and sustainable energy are set out in the Your World chapter.

your life. Liberal Democrats believe in investing in and improving the quality of our public services. They are the cornerstone of a fair society, opening up opportunities and providing support and help when needed.

change that works **for you**
BUILDING A FAIRER BRITAIN

a fair deal and the help you need from public services

Liberal Democrats believe in investing in and improving the quality of our public services. They are the cornerstone of a fair society, opening up opportunities and providing support and help when needed.

Despite increased investment, there are still problems. Too many children leave school without the knowledge and skills to be successful. The NHS often feels too remote and complex for patients to handle, while doctors and nurses spend too much time trying to meet government targets. And inequality is rife: in Britain today your chances in life are more determined by your parents' income than anywhere else in the developed world.

We will provide **a fair start for all children** by giving schools the extra money they need to **cut class sizes** and provide additional one-to-one teaching, and by setting schools free to give all children the best possible education. We will **scrap unfair university tuition fees** so everyone has the chance to get a degree, regardless of their parents' income. We will help the NHS work better with the money it has by using **the savings we have found to protect front-line services**, such as cancer treatment, mental health care, maternity services, dementia care and preventive medicine.

the best chance for every child

Liberal Democrats want every child to receive an excellent education, to unlock children's potential and to ensure that they can succeed in life.

Too many children are still leaving school without the knowledge and skills to be successful. And your family background still has a huge effect: a typical child from a poor family will fall behind a richer classmate by the age of seven and never catch up. We will seek to ensure that all pupils leaving primary and secondary education have the skills they need.

We will free schools from the present stranglehold of central government control and encourage them to be genuinely innovative.

We will invest additional money in the schools system to allow schools to cut class sizes, pay for one-to-one tuition, introduce catch-up classes, or take other steps to ensure that every child has the best possible education.

We will therefore ensure that every neighbourhood is served by an excellent local school or college.

We will:

- Increase the funding of the most disadvantaged pupils, around one million children. We will invest £2.5 billion in this 'Pupil Premium' to boost education opportunities for every child. This is additional money going into the schools budget, and headteachers will be free to spend it in the best interests of children.

- The extra money could be used to cut class sizes, attract the best teachers, offer extra one-to-one tuition and provide for after-school and holiday support. This will allow an average primary school to cut classes to 20 and an average secondary school to introduce catch-up classes for 160 pupils.

- Improve discipline by early intervention to tackle the poor basic education of those children who are otherwise most likely to misbehave and become demotivated.

- Guarantee Special Educational Needs (SEN) diagnostic assessments for all 5-year-olds, improve SEN provision and improve SEN training for teachers.

- Improve teacher training by increasing the size of the school-based Graduate Teacher Programme and support the expansion of Teach

First to attract more top graduates into teaching. We will improve training for existing teachers over the course of their careers to keep them up to date with best practice. We will seek to ensure that science at Key Stage 4 and above is taught by appropriately qualified teachers.

- Confront bullying, including homophobic bullying, and include bullying prevention in teacher training.

- Set aside extra money for schools to improve the energy efficiency of their buildings. They will pay back the loan over time from energy savings, creating a rolling fund to help insulate other public buildings.

a better education: standards and the curriculum

To make the most of their years at school, every child needs an education tailored to suit their abilities and interests. The restrictive National Curriculum and the arbitrary split between academic and vocational qualifications isn't working.

We will:

- Establish a fully independent Educational Standards Authority (ESA) with real powers to stand up to ministers and restore confidence in standards. The ESA would oversee the examinations system, the systems of school inspection and accountability, and the detail of the curriculum. It would replace the Qualifications and Curriculum Development Agency and the Office of the Qualifications and Examinations Regulator (OFQUAL), and include OFSTED, the schools inspectorate.

- Replace the bureaucratic Early Years Foundation Stage with a slimmed-down framework which includes a range of educational approaches and enough flexibility for every young child.

- Axe the rigid National Curriculum, and replace it with a slimmed down 'Minimum Curriculum Entitlement' to be delivered by every state-funded school.

- Scale back Key Stage 2 tests at age 11, and use teacher assessment, with external checking, to improve the quality of marking.

- Create a General Diploma to bring GCSEs, A-Levels and high quality vocational qualifications together, enabling pupils to mix vocational and academic learning.

- Give 14–19 year-olds the right to take up a course at college, rather than at school, if it suits them better. This will enable all children to choose to study, for example, separate sciences or modern languages at GCSE, or a vocational subject.

- Seek to close the unfair funding gap between pupils in school sixth forms and Further Education colleges, as resources allow.

- Scrap the Government's plan to criminalise those who leave education between ages 16 and 18.

- Reform league tables to give parents more meaningful information which truly reflects the performance of a school. Schools should be working to get the best from all their pupils but government league tables are forcing them to focus on those who are just above or below the key C-grade borderline.

freeing schools for excellence

Liberal Democrats want an education system where all schools will have the freedom to innovate, not be dictated to by central government.

We will:

- Introduce an Education Freedom Act banning politicians from getting involved in the day-to-day running of schools. Teachers are held back by constant government interference which distracts from teaching. We would cut the size of the central department of Children, Schools and Families, and focus its activities on a few strategic priorities. Local authorities will not run schools, but will have a central strategic role, including responsibility for oversight of school performance and fair admissions. They will be expected to intervene where school leadership or performance is weak.

- Give all schools the freedom to innovate. We will ensure a level playing field for admissions and funding and replace Academies with our own model of 'Sponsor-Managed Schools'. These schools will be commissioned by and accountable to local authorities and not Whitehall, and would allow other appropriate providers, such as educational charities and parent groups, to be involved in delivering state-funded education.

- Allow parents to continue to choose faith-based schools within the state-funded sector and allow the establishment of new faith schools. We will ensure that all faith schools develop an inclusive admissions policy and end unfair discrimination on grounds of faith when recruiting staff, except for those principally responsible for optional religious instruction.

- Reform the existing rigid national pay and conditions rules to give schools and colleges more freedom, including in offering financial and other incentives to attract and retain excellent teachers, while ensuring that all staff receive the minimum national pay award.

opportunities at college and university

There should be a wide range of opportunities for everyone at the age of 16. Liberal Democrats believe that education is important for all young people, and will create, finally, a level playing field between academic and vocational courses. And we will ensure that adults who wish to study, including those wanting to return to education later on in life, are able to do so without being put off by the burden of debt. We will:

- Scrap unfair university tuition fees for all students taking their first degree, including those studying part-time, saving them over £10,000 each. We have a financially responsible plan to phase fees out over six years, so that the change is affordable even in these difficult economic times, and without cutting university income. We will immediately scrap fees for final year students.

- Reform current bursary schemes to create a National Bursary Scheme for students, so that each university gets a bursary budget suited to the needs of its students. These bursaries would be awarded both on the basis of studying strategic subjects (such as sciences and mathematics) and financial hardship.

- Replace wasteful quangos (the Skills Funding Agency and the Higher Education Funding Council for England) with a single Council for Adult Skills and Higher Education.

- Scrap the arbitrary target of 50 per cent of young people attending university, focussing effort instead on a balance of college education, vocational training and apprenticeships.

- Start discussions with universities and schools about the design of a trial scheme whereby the best students from the lowest achieving schools are guaranteed a place in Higher Education.

- As part of our immediate job creation package, fund 15,000 new places on Foundation Degree courses and fully fund the off-the-job costs of adult apprenticeships, which currently have to be met by employers, for one year.

- Better target spending on adult skills. We will end Train to Gain funding for large companies, restricting the funds to the small and medium-sized firms that need the support. The money saved will be used to cover the course fees for adults taking a first Level 3 qualification (such as A-levels or an adult apprenticeship), allowing a significant reduction in the overall budget.

protecting and improving our NHS

We are proud of the NHS – it's built on the basic British principle of fairness. Liberal Democrats believe that we can improve the NHS; in fact, we believe it's our duty to do so at a time like this when budgets are tight. We all know that too much precious NHS money is wasted on bureaucracy, and doctors and nurses spend too much time trying to meet government targets.

So our first priority is to increase spending in some parts of the NHS by cutting waste in others. We have identified specific savings that can be made in management costs, bureaucracy and quangos, and we will reinvest that money back into the health care you need. Because of the rising costs of treatments and an ageing population, there will be particular pressure on services like cancer treatment, mental health care, maternity services, and dementia care; only by going through this process of finding savings elsewhere can we protect these services in the coming years. The NHS is a huge system, and we will make changes to ensure it works as effectively as possible.

We will:

- Give priority to preventing people getting ill by linking payments to health boards and GPs more directly to prevention measures.

- Cut the size of the Department of Health by half, abolish unnecessary quangos such as Connecting for Health and cut the budgets of the rest, scrap Strategic Health Authorities and seek to limit the pay and bonuses of top NHS managers so that none are paid more than the Prime Minister.

- Make the NHS work better by extending best practice on improving hospital discharge, maximising the number of day case operations, reducing delays prior to operations, and where possible moving consultations into the community.

- Integrate health and social care to create a seamless service, ending bureaucratic barriers and saving money to allow people to stay in their homes for longer rather than going into hospital or long-term residential care.

- Use the money for Labour's flawed Personal Care At Home Bill to provide guaranteed respite care for the one million carers who work the longest hours. We will establish an independent commission, with cross-party support, to develop proposals for long-term care of the elderly.

- Prioritise dementia research within the health research and development budget.

- Improve access to counselling for people with mental health problems, by continuing the roll-out of cognitive and behavioural therapies.

- Reduce the ill health and crime caused by excessive drinking. We support a ban on below-cost selling, and are in favour of the principle of minimum pricing, subject to detailed work to establish how it could be used in tackling problems of irresponsible drinking. We will also review the complex, ill-thought-through system of taxation for alcohol to ensure it tackles binge drinking without unfairly penalising responsible drinkers, pubs and important local industries.

- Save lives and reduce pressure on NHS budgets by cutting air pollution. We will cancel plans for a third runway at Heathrow and other airport expansion in the South East, and reduce pollution from vehicle exhausts through tighter regulation. We will aim to fully meet European air quality targets by 2012.

more control over the health care you need

Liberal Democrats believe that one important way to improve the NHS is to make care flexible, designed to suit what patients need, not what managers want. And we believe that care would improve if local people had more control over how their health services were run.

The NHS often feels too remote and complex. Local services – especially maternity wards and accident and emergency departments – keep being closed, even though local people desperately want them to stay open. People often struggle to get convenient access to GP services, and poorer areas are less well served by the NHS, contributing to widening health inequalities.

We will change this by:

- Sharply reducing centralised targets and bureaucracy, replacing them with entitlements guaranteeing that patients get diagnosis and treatment on time. If they do not, the NHS will pay for the treatment to be provided privately.

- Putting front-line staff in charge of their ward or unit budgets, and allowing staff to establish employee trusts giving them real involvement and a say over how their service is run.

- Empowering local communities to improve health services through elected Local Health Boards, which will take over the role of Primary Care Trust boards in commissioning care for local people, working in co-operation with local councils. Over time, Local Health Boards should be able to take on greater responsibility for revenue and resources to allow local people to fund local services which need extra money.

- Giving every patient the right to choose to register with the GP they want, without being restricted by where they live, and the right to access their GP by email.

- Ensuring that local GPs are directly involved in providing out-of-hours care.

- Reforming payments to GPs so that those who accept patients from areas with the worst health and deprivation scores receive an extra payment for each one they take.

- Giving Local Health Boards the freedom to commission services for local people from a range of different types of provider, including for example staff co-operatives, on the basis of a level playing field in any competitive tendering – ending any current bias in favour of private providers.

quality care for all patients

We all need to be assured that, if we become unwell, the care we get will be of good quality. Most of all, we need to be confident that our safety comes first, and that the treatment we get doesn't put us in more danger. We will introduce a series of reforms to improve patient safety.

We will:

- Require hospitals to be open about mistakes, and always tell patients if something has gone wrong.

- Make it illegal for a Local Health Board to allow a doctor to work in the UK without passing robust language and competence tests.

- Clamp down on anyone who is aggressive or abusive to staff in accident and emergency departments. We would encourage better working relationships between hospitals and the local police to provide an increased police presence at times of high risk, and increase prosecutions. At the same time, we will ensure that problem drinkers or substance abusers are referred for appropriate treatment.

It is deeply disappointing that the Government has failed to provide adequate support for those affected by the contamination of blood products with HIV. A Liberal Democrat government will establish a working group involving patient groups to determine appropriate levels of financial assistance.

access to culture and sport

Liberal Democrats believe that the arts are a central part of civic and community life. They contribute to innovation, education, diversity, and social inclusion, and the creative industries are one of the fastest growing sectors of the economy. Britain's culture and heritage play a vital role in attracting visitors to the UK and boosting the very important tourism industry. We will foster an environment in which all forms of creativity are able to flourish.

We are proud that Britain is hosting the Olympic and Paralympic Games in 2012, and we support bids for other high-profile events such as the 2018 World Cup – but we believe that grassroots sport is just as important. We

will give people from all backgrounds and generations the opportunity to participate in sports.

Liberal Democrats will:

- Maintain free entry to national museums and galleries and open up the Government Art Collection for greater public use.

- Set up a 'Creative Enterprise Fund' offering training, mentoring and small grants or loans to help creative businesses get off the ground.

- Cut red tape for putting on live music. We will reintroduce the rule allowing two performers of unamplified music in any licensed premises without the need for an entertainment licence, allow licensed venues for up to 200 people to host live music without the need for an entertainment licence, and remove the requirement for schools and hospitals to apply for a licence.

- Reform the National Lottery. We will change the way the National Lottery is taxed from a ticket tax to a gross profits tax, which is forecast to deliver more for good causes and the Exchequer.

- Use cash in dormant betting accounts to set up a capital fund for improving local sports facilities and supporting sports clubs.

- Close loopholes that allow playing fields to be sold or built upon without going through the normal planning procedures.

A strong and diverse media, free from government interference and pressure is essential to a free and democratic society. We will:

- Ensure that the BBC remains strong, free from interference and securely funded, not least to provide impartial news, independent of political and commercial pressures. We will also ensure that the BBC does not undermine the viability of other media providers through unfair competition based on its public funding and dominant position.

- Support a diverse regional and local media. We will help to maintain independent local sources of news and information by enabling partnerships between TV, radio and newspaper companies to reduce costs, and by limiting publicly-subsidised competition for paid advertising from local council free-sheets.

your life

your family. In Britain today, families come in all shapes and sizes. Liberal Democrats believe every family should get the support it needs to thrive.

change that works **for you**

BUILDING A FAIRER BRITAIN

a fair deal for families of every shape and size

In Britain today, families come in all shapes and sizes. Liberal Democrats believe every family should get the support it needs to thrive, from help with childcare through to better support for carers and elderly parents.

Liberal Democrats will improve life for your family. On top of our tax cuts to put £700 in the pockets of millions of low and middle-income earners, we will allow **mums and dads to share parental leave between them** so they can arrange family life in the way that suits them best. We will provide **better support for children at risk** and young adults to help them thrive. We will **restore the earnings link** for pensions, and offer **respite breaks for carers**. And we will **protect families from unfair bills**.

help for families – right from the start

The first weeks, months and years after a child is born are enormously important, but the support arrangements are simply too inflexible at the moment. When a baby is born, the mother gets a year's leave and the father gets just two weeks, meaning the mother has to take the lion's share of the responsibility, even if their partner would rather share things more equally.

Liberal Democrats will:

- Give fathers the right to time off for ante-natal appointments.

- Allow parents to share the allocation of maternity and paternity leave between them in whatever way suits them best.

- Protect existing childcare support arrangements until the nation's finances can support a longer term solution: a move to 20 hours free childcare for every child, from the age of 18 months.

- Seek to extend the period of shared parental leave up to 18 months when resources and economic circumstances allow.

- Support efforts by childcare providers to encourage more men to work in this hugely important and undervalued profession.

- Extend the right to request flexible working to all employees, making it easier for grandparents, for example, to take a caring role.

helping families stay strong

Every child deserves a happy life free from poverty and free from fear. Children face too many difficulties in today's Britain; the Government is going to fall far short of its target to cut child poverty, and young people have been demonised by a generation of politicians more interested in sounding tough than in offering help. Children are also the main victims of family breakdown.

Liberal Democrats will:

- Maintain the commitment to end child poverty in the UK by 2020.

- Incorporate the UN Convention on the Rights of the Child into UK law, ending the detention of children for immigration purposes.

- Enhance child protection. We will enforce the publication of an anonymised version of Serious Case Reviews to ensure that lessons are learned.

- Support the objective of at least a 70 per cent reduction in child maltreatment by 2030, promoted by the WAVE trust.

- Help protect children and young people from developing negative body images by regulating airbrushing in adverts.

- Tackle online bullying by backing quick-report buttons on social networking sites, enabling offensive postings to be speedily removed.

- Strengthen the Youth Service by making it a statutory service, and by encouraging local authorities to provide youth services in partnership with young people and the voluntary sector.

- Set the minimum wage at the same level for all workers over 16 (except for those on apprenticeships).

- Introduce a Default Contact Arrangement which would divide the child's time between their two parents in the event of family breakdown, if there is no threat to the safety of the child.

dignity and security in later life

The way older people are treated is the mark of a fair society. Older people have worked hard and contributed to society for decades; they deserve a fair deal. Liberal Democrats will increase the inadequate basic state pension and ensure fair treatment for everyone from government, public services and business alike.

That is why Liberal Democrats will:

- Immediately restore the link between the basic state pension and earnings. We will uprate the state pension annually by whichever is the higher of growth in earnings, growth in prices or 2.5 per cent.

- Increase the income tax threshold to £10,000, saving most pensioners around £100 a year.

- Offer a week's respite for the one million carers who spend 50 hours every week looking after a sick relative.

- Scrap compulsory retirement ages, allowing those who wish to continue in work to do so.

- Give you control over your own pension by scrapping the rules that compel you to buy an annuity when you reach 75.

- In the long term, aim to bring in a Citizen's Pension that will be paid to all UK citizens who are long-term residents, set at the level of the

Pension Credit, though this can only be done when resources allow.

- Begin a national programme to insulate many more homes paid for by the savings from lower energy bills.

There is a further, serious, long-term crisis facing older people: the sustainability of the systems for providing long-term care. It is unacceptable that this challenge has been treated as a political football. A Liberal Democrat Government would immediately establish an independent commission to develop future proposals for long-term care that will attract all-party support and so be sustainable. We believe that the eventual solution must be based on the principles of fairness, affordability and sustainability.

a fair deal for consumers

While open markets usually deliver opportunity and prosperity, sometimes markets fail and consumers are badly treated by big business. The banks have exploited their position of power to impose unfair charges. Energy bills are far too expensive for many people, and suppliers have not done enough to protect those who cannot afford to keep warm.

We will:

- Change the tariffs used by energy supply companies so that the first, essential, energy you use is the cheapest. We'll ensure that effective energy efficiency measures are introduced to keep bills low and that 'social tariffs' are available to guarantee the best price for all those in most need. We will seek to extend protection and support to 'off-gas-grid' consumers.

- Address unfairness in water charges by consulting on the implementation of the Walker Review which recommended action to deal with regional unfairness in water charges.

- Legislate to end unfair bank and financial transaction charges, so you cannot be charged more than the costs incurred.

- Improve access to banking for all with a PostBank, revenues from which will also help to secure the future of the Post Office.

- Impose maximum interest rates for credit cards and store cards, following consultation with the financial industry and consumer groups.

- Introduce a Universal Service Code to secure high-quality customer service in the private and public sectors, for example by requiring that the customer service phone number is free from mobiles and landlines.

- Require a local competition test for all planning applications for new retail developments and establish a local competition office within the Office of Fair Trading to investigate anti-competitive practices at a local and regional level.

- Require airlines to be honest and upfront about pricing, ending the practice of adding hidden charges.

- Cut rail fares, changing the rules in contracts with Train Operating Companies so that regulated fares fall behind inflation by 1 per cent each year, meaning a real-terms cut.

- Make Network Rail refund a third of your ticket price if you have to take a rail replacement bus service.

- Regulate the parking system to remove unfairness and stop private sector wheel-clamping.

your family

enhanced protection for animals

Liberal Democrats believe that ownership and use of animals is a
responsibility that should not be abused.

We will:

- Merge existing quangos to establish an Animal Protection Commission
  to investigate abuses, educate the public and enforce the law; it will
  also be able to publish reports on its own initiative.

- End testing of household products on animals.

- Work for the proper enforcement of regulations for the transportation
  of live animals across all EU member states.

your world. Britain must work together with our partners abroad if we are to have the best hope of meeting the challenges the world faces. We believe in freedom, justice, prosperity and human rights for all and will do all we can to work towards a world where these hopes become reality. Above all, climate change is the greatest challenge facing this generation.

change that works **for you**

BUILDING A FAIRER BRITAIN

securing Britain's future with global action

Liberal Democrats believe that Britain must work together with its partners abroad if we are to have the best hope of meeting the challenges the world faces. We believe in freedom, justice, prosperity and human rights for all and will do all we can to work towards a world where these hopes become reality.

Never has there been such a need for global action. There are only a few years to take action to stop runaway climate change. The global recession proved the need for better international regulation of the financial markets. New security threats are emerging, for which Britain's armed forces are not yet fully equipped, whilst terrorists and organised criminals exploit international networks. The challenge of tackling global poverty remains, with the Millennium Development Goals still far from being achieved. And the battle for human rights remains to be fought in many countries.

Liberal Democrats will work through the European Union to deliver **a global deal on climate change**. We will transform the armed forces, meeting the nation's obligations under the **military covenant**, and conducting **a full defence review** to ensure they are equipped for modern threats. We will push for **better global financial regulation**. We will strive for global nuclear disarmament, showing leadership by **committing not to replace the Trident nuclear weapons system** on a like-for-like basis. We will meet the UK's obligations to the developing world by committing to spending **0.7 per cent of GNI on aid**. And we will put **Britain at the heart of Europe**, to ensure we use our influence to achieve prosperity, security and opportunity for Britain.

tackling climate change

Climate change is the greatest challenge facing this generation. Liberal Democrats are unwavering in our commitment: runaway climate change must be stopped, and politicians must follow the science in order to make that happen.

We will set a target for a zero-carbon Britain that doesn't contribute at all to global warming – making the British economy carbon-neutral overall by 2050, reducing carbon emissions in the UK by over 40 per cent of 1990 levels by 2020 as a step on the way.

Our response to climate change will give the British people more secure energy supplies, reduce air pollution and related health costs – and create thousands of new jobs.

Liberal Democrats will:

- Begin a ten-year programme of home insulation, offering a home energy improvement package of up to £10,000 per home, paid for by the savings from lower energy bills, and make sure every new home is fully energy-efficient by improving building regulations.

- Set a target for 40 per cent of UK electricity to come from clean, non-carbon-emitting sources by 2020, rising to 100 per cent by 2050, underpinned by guaranteed price support; and ensure that at least three-quarters of this new renewable energy comes from marine and offshore sources.

- Set out a clear renewables routemap to 2050, covering grid access and investment in electricity networks, and develop new incentives to promote renewable heat.

- Transform the electricity networks into a dynamic electricity grid that can better connect and integrate new, clean energy technologies particularly through the better use of sub-sea connections, leading to the development of a European Supergrid.

- Invest up to £400 million in refurbishing shipyards in the North of

England and Scotland so that they can manufacture offshore wind turbines and other marine renewable energy equipment.

- Launch an 'Eco Cash-Back' scheme, for one year only, which will give you £400 if you install double glazing, replace an old boiler, or install micro-generation. If you choose micro-generation, you will be able to sell the energy back to the National Grid at a profit, with a more attractive feed-in tariff than under current government plans.

- Set aside extra money for schools to improve the energy efficiency of their buildings. They will pay back the loan over time from energy savings, creating a rolling fund to help insulate all public buildings.

- Invest £140 million in a bus scrappage scheme that helps bus companies to replace old polluting buses with new low-carbon ones and creates jobs.

- Block any new coal-fired power stations – the most polluting form of power generation – unless they are accompanied by the highest level of carbon capture and storage facilities.

- Reject a new generation of nuclear power stations; based on the evidence nuclear is a far more expensive way of reducing carbon emissions than promoting energy conservation and renewable energy.

- Improve energy efficiency in the commercial and public sectors, by strengthening the Carbon Reduction Commitment Energy Efficiency Scheme and requiring companies and government departments to report on their energy use and set targets for reducing it. We will set a 30 per cent energy efficiency improvement target for 2020, and will commit the government to the goals of the 10:10 campaign as a first step.

leading the fight against climate change

Liberal Democrats are committed to securing a legally binding global agreement on limiting the increase in global temperatures to below 1.7 degrees Celsius. We believe that such an agreement must be based on reducing emissions overall, while equalising emissions between the developed and developing worlds – the principle of contraction and convergence. Strong and credible EU ambition, with effective UK leadership, are essential for achieving a global agreement, so that total greenhouse gas emissions peak no later than 2015. Liberal Democrats will work within Europe and internationally to give renewed urgency to global efforts to combat climate change.

We will press the EU to:

- Promote the transition to a low-carbon economy in Europe, by moving unilaterally and immediately to an EU emissions reduction target of 30 per cent by 2020, adopting new long-term targets and policies for clean energy and energy efficiency; and expand investment in energy technology innovation, within Europe and internationally.

- Boost investment in clean energy by reforming the EU emissions trading scheme – bringing in a tighter cap on emissions, auctioning as many allowances as possible, and encouraging other European countries to increase the use of reserve prices in allowance auctions.

- Engage with major emitters and deepen diplomatic co-operation between the EU and emerging economies and developing countries, provide enhanced financial support for low-carbon solutions and lead international efforts to promote the transfer of technologies that will help to tackle climate change.

- Work for the adoption of 'quick win' measures that could be initiated within the next few years such as reducing the use of hydrofluorocarbons (HFCs).

At the UN level, we will support the provision of UN Adaptation Funds for developing countries, financed from international emissions markets, such as a cap-and-trade system for international emissions from aviation and shipping.

protecting the global environment

Humans are living beyond the ability of the planet to support life; more than 60 per cent of the basic ecosystems that support life on Earth are being degraded or used unsustainably. Co-ordinated international action and effective global institutions are necessary to help create a sustainable future and improve the quality of life of all the world's citizens.

Liberal Democrats will:

- Work through the EU to make sure that the environment is fully integrated into the objectives of international institutions such as the World Bank, International Monetary Fund and World Trade Organisation.

- Work to increase the resourcing of the UN Environment Programme and improve the enforcement of international environmental treaties.

- Protect the world's forests, not only to reduce carbon emissions but also to preserve this crucial reservoir of biodiversity. We will argue for an international target of zero net deforestation by 2020; support a new system of payments to developing countries to enable them to reduce deforestation; and adopt at EU – or, if necessary, at UK – level a new law making it illegal to import or possess timber produced illegally in foreign countries.

- Work with other countries to develop an international labelling system for the environmental impact of products, helping consumers choose those with the least impact on resource use and pollution.

meeting Britain's obligations to the developing world

Liberal Democrats are committed to working towards a world free from poverty, inequality and injustice and meeting the Millennium Development Goals is a vital first step. But beyond this we will also ensure that action is taken to allow developing nations to grow and to prevent them suffering unfairly the effects of climate change inflicted by developed countries.

Liberal Democrats will:

- Increase the UK's aid budget to reach the UN target of 0.7 per cent of GNI by 2013 and enshrine that target in law. We will hold the G8 to its Gleneagles pledges on aid, including on the 0.7 per cent target.

- Work with other countries to establish new sources of development financing, including bringing forward urgent proposals for a financial transaction tax and a cap-and-trade system for carbon emissions from aviation and shipping.

- Support reform of the global financial institutions such as the World Bank and IMF.

- Ban banks from facilitating the transfer of funds obtained by corruption. We will crack down on tax havens which allow individuals and corporations to avoid paying taxes to developing countries.

- Ensure that the developing world is prepared to deal with the consequences of a changing climate. We will ensure that adaptation and mitigation measures are financed by industrialised nations on top of existing aid commitments.

- Prioritise health and education programmes which aim to promote gender equality, reduce maternal and infant mortality, and restrict the spread of major diseases like HIV/AIDS, TB and malaria. We will focus effort on supplying basic needs like clean water.

- Support a global fund for social protection to help developing countries build viable welfare systems.

- Push for a renewed international effort on debt and support 100 per cent cancellation of the unpayable debts of the world's poorest countries. We will also take measures against 'vulture funds' and lobby for similar action at international level.

equipping Britain's armed forces for the 21st century

Modern armed forces face a series of complex challenges. Alongside fighting conventional wars, they seek to protect us from the threats of terrorism, maintain the peace, undertake conflict prevention and help facilitate development in poorer nations.

The world has changed enormously since the end of the Cold War. New threats are emerging and yet Britain's armed forces remain largely equipped to fight the old ones. The Iraq War, and allegations over British complicity in torture and in secret 'rendition' flights of terrorist suspects, highlight the dangers of a subservient relationship with the United States that neglects Britain's core values and interests.

The threats of tomorrow are likely to be driven by failed states, mass migration, climate change and regional instability. So we will ensure that taxpayers' money is spent more effectively on equipping the forces for the tasks of the future, not old Cold War threats. We will:

- Hold an immediate Strategic Security and Defence Review (SSDR) to ensure that Britain deploys its resources to face the most serious threats to its citizens' security and well-being, including non-military challenges such as climate change.

- With strong Treasury involvement, review all major defence procurement projects through the SSDR to ensure money is being spent effectively. We will not purchase tranche 3B of the Eurofighter.

- Rule out the like-for-like replacement of the Trident nuclear weapons system. At a cost of £100 billion over a lifetime it is unaffordable, and Britain's security would be better served by alternatives. We support multilateral nuclear disarmament and will ensure that the UK plays a proactive role in the arms reduction talks starting later this year.

- Reinvigorate Franco-British and wider European defence co-operation to ensure procurement costs are kept low.

a fair deal for our service personnel

The brave men and women of Britain's armed forces are the most precious military asset we have. They must be treated fairly, with pay and conditions that reflect their outstanding commitment to this country, and properly valued and supported after they leave the services.

Liberal Democrats will put the forces' welfare first. We will:

- Give a pay rise to the lower ranks so that their pay is brought into line with the starting salary of their emergency services counterparts.

- Double the rate of modernisation of forces' family homes to ensure they are fit for heroes.

While it is necessary to find resources to support the troops properly, at the same time fairness requires that we make savings where possible within the defence budget as a whole. We will reduce the number of civilian staff in the Ministry of Defence and reduce numbers of top brass officers.

putting Britain at the heart of Europe

Liberal Democrats believe that European co-operation is the best way for Britain to be strong, safe and influential in the future. We will ensure that Britain maximises its influence through a strong and positive commitment.

But just because Europe is essential, that doesn't mean the European Union is perfect. We will continue to campaign for improved accountability, efficiency and effectiveness. Working together, the member states of the EU have a better chance of managing the impacts of globalisation, such as cross-border crime and environmental pollution.

Liberal Democrats will:

- Work with Britain's European neighbours to create thousands of new jobs by breaking down trade barriers and boosting support for green jobs.

- Work through the European Union for stricter international regulation of financial services and banking.

- Keep Britain part of international crime-fighting measures such as the European Arrest Warrant, European Police Office (Europol), Eurojust, and the European Criminal Records Information System, while ensuring high standards of justice.

- Keep the pressure on for reform of agricultural subsidies so that farmers, consumers and taxpayers get a fair deal, and the environment is protected.

- Fight to stop MEPs having to travel to the Strasbourg Parliament every month, wasting €200 million a year.

- Campaign for continuing reform of the EU budget so that money is spent only on the things the EU really needs to do.

The European Union has evolved significantly since the last public vote on membership over thirty years ago. Liberal Democrats therefore remain committed to an in/out referendum the next time a British government signs up for fundamental change in the relationship between the UK and the EU.

We believe that it is in Britain's long-term interest to be part of the euro. But Britain should only join when the economic conditions are right, and in the present economic situation, they are not. Britain should join the euro only if that decision were supported by the people of Britain in a referendum.

standing up for liberal values around the world

Liberal Democrats will put British values of fairness and the rule of law back at the heart of our foreign policy. British people used to be proud of what our country stood for. But Britain's reputation has been damaged by unscrupulous arms deals with dictators, allegations of involvement in torture, and of course the disastrous and illegal invasion of Iraq. We will also give greater support to conflict prevention – which saves money and saves lives.

We will:

- Make the EU use its collective weight effectively in other areas of foreign policy. Britain can have a far stronger voice on relations with Russia, China, Iran and the Middle East peace process when it joins with the rest of Europe.

- Be critical supporters of the Afghanistan mission. The military surge must be accompanied by a strategy to ensure a more legitimate government, tackle corruption and win over moderate elements in the insurgency. We will continue to demand a strategy that involves other players in the region. We believe that a successful strategy will stabilise Afghanistan enough to allow British troops to come home during the next Parliament.

- Support the establishment of an International Arms Trade Treaty to limit the sale of arms to dangerous regimes and work for a full international ban on cluster munitions. We will ensure that British arms are not sold to states that would use them for internal repression. We will require arms brokers to register under a code of conduct and revoke the licences of those who break the code.

- Support action by the international community to stop Iran obtaining nuclear weapons. We would follow a diplomatic route of active engagement, and are ready to back targeted sanctions, but we oppose military action against Iran and believe those calling for such action undermine the growing reform movement in Iran.

- Hold a full judicial inquiry into allegations of British complicity in torture and state kidnapping as part of a process to restore Britain's reputation for decency and fairness.

- Remain committed to the search for a peaceful resolution of the Israeli-Palestinian conflict. A sustainable solution can be reached in the context of two separate Israeli and Palestinian states, mutually recognised and internationally accepted within borders which are secure and based on the situation before the 1967 conflict. We condemn disproportionate force used by all sides. We believe Britain and the EU must put pressure on Israel and Egypt to end the blockade of Gaza.

your world

your community. Liberal Democrats believe in strong communities, where local people can come together to meet local needs, enjoy a pleasant local environment, and feel free from the threat of crime.

rebuilding security, opportunity, homes and hope

Liberal Democrats believe in strong communities, where local people can come together to meet local needs, enjoy a pleasant local environment, and feel free from the threat of crime. We want every community to be safe and fair, and offer opportunities to people of every background.

Under Labour and Conservative rule, communities have been let down. Governments have talked tough on crime but failed to take effective action. Lack of affordable housing has driven many young people out of the communities where they were born. Public transport is expensive when it is there at all. Key local services like the Post Office have declined dramatically.

Liberal Democrats will **put thousands more police on the beat** and make them work more effectively to cut crime. We value Britain's open, welcoming character, and will protect it by **changing the immigration system to make it firm and fair** so that people can once again put their faith in it. We will invest in public transport and **cut rail fares**, as well as **providing more affordable homes** and protecting people from unfair repossessions. We will **keep post offices open**, and will **protect and restore the natural environment**.

cutting crime with more and better police

We will focus on what works to cut crime. We will support more positive activities for young people to stop them getting involved in a life of crime. Labour and the Conservatives posture on penalties, which do not deter criminals. What does deter them is increasing the chances of being caught. That is why more police are needed on the streets – to provide a longer arm for the law. And we need to help the police to be more effective at catching criminals, spend less time on bureaucracy and more time preventing crime, reassuring the public and helping keep everyone safe.

Liberal Democrats will:

- Pay for 3,000 more police on the beat, affordable because we are cutting other spending, such as scrapping pointless ID cards.

- Reduce time-wasting bureaucracy at police stations with better technology that can be deployed on the streets.

- Give local people a real say over their police force through the direct election of police authorities. Authorities would still be able to co-opt extra members to ensure diversity, experience and expertise.

- Give far more power to elected police authorities, including the right to sack and appoint the Chief Constable, set local policing priorities, and agree and determine budgets.

- Strengthen the Youth Service by making it a statutory service, and encourage local authorities to provide youth services in partnership with young people and the voluntary sector.

- Reform the police, with a full review of the very restrictive terms and conditions for police officer employment.

- Turn the National Policing Improvement Agency into a National Crime Reduction Agency with a wider remit to test what policing techniques and sentences work and spread best practice across police services and the criminal justice system.

practical steps to make you safer

We will do all we can to prevent crime with practical measures that we know will make a difference and keep people safe.

We will:

- Make hospitals share non-confidential information with the police so they know where gun and knife crime is happening and can target stop-and-search in gun and knife crime hot spots.

- Bring in stop-on-request for night buses. You should be able to ask the driver to let you off between stops, so you're as close to home as possible.

- Require better recording of hate crimes against disabled, homosexual and transgender people, which are frequently not centrally recorded.

- Ensure that financial resources, and police and court time, are not wasted on the unnecessary prosecution and imprisonment of drug users and addicts; the focus instead should be on getting addicts

the treatment they need. Police should concentrate their efforts on organised drug pushers and gangs.

- Always base drugs policy on independent scientific advice, including making the Advisory Council on the Misuse of Drugs completely independent of government.

making the justice system work to rehabilitate criminals and reduce crime

Liberal Democrats believe that once a criminal has been caught, it is vital that the punishment they are given helps to turn them away from crime, and set them back on the straight and narrow.

Too many politicians have talked tough, meting out ever-longer prison sentences, but doing far too little to tackle reoffending and to stop crime happening in the first place. As a result, the government is spending more and more on prisons, but those released from them are as likely as ever to commit more crimes. We will:

- Make prisoners work and contribute from their prison wages to a compensation fund for victims. As resources allow, we will increase the number of hours prisoners spend in education and training.

- Introduce a presumption against short-term sentences of less than six months – replaced by rigorously enforced community sentences which evidence shows are better at cutting reoffending.

- Move offenders who are drug addicts or mentally ill into more appropriate secure accommodation.

- As a consequence of these changes, be able to cancel the Government's billion-pound prison building programme.

- Give people a direct say in how petty criminals and those who engage in anti-social behaviour are punished by setting up Neighbourhood Justice Panels (NJPs), like the one run by Liberal Democrats in Somerset where 95 per cent of offenders have been turned away from further crimes.

- Champion restorative justice programmes, like NJPs, which make offenders confront their behaviour and are more successful at reducing crime than traditional forms of punishment.

firm but fair immigration system

Britain has always been an open, welcoming country, and thousands of businesses, schools and hospitals in many parts of the country rely on people who've come to live here from overseas. It would be wrong to try and end immigration completely but we have to manage migration so that it benefits Britain and is fair for everyone.

The immigration system is in chaos after decades of incompetent management. The Government has failed to plan properly for new migrants, making it harder for people to integrate. No-one has any idea how many people are here illegally, and there aren't even exit checks at all ports and airports to ensure that people here on temporary visas go home on time.

We will create a fair system that works and promotes integration. We will:

- Immediately reintroduce exit checks at all ports and airports.

- Secure Britain's borders by giving a National Border Force police powers.

- Introduce a regional points-based system to ensure that migrants can work only where they are needed. We need to enforce any immigration system through rigorous checks on businesses and a crackdown on rogue employers who profit from illegal labour.

- Prioritise deportation efforts on criminals, people-traffickers and other high-priority cases. We will let law-abiding families earn citizenship. We will allow people who have been in Britain without the correct papers for ten years, but speak English, have a clean record and want to live here long-term to earn their citizenship. This route to citizenship will not apply to people arriving after 2010.

a safe haven for those fleeing persecution

Britain has a responsibility to welcome refugees fleeing wars and persecution around the world. Liberal Democrats will abide by Britain's international obligations and restore confidence in the asylum system by making it firm and fair.

We will:

- Take responsibility for asylum away from the Home Office and give it to a wholly independent agency, as has been successful in Canada.

- Push for a co-ordinated EU-wide asylum system to ensure that the responsibility is fairly shared between member states.

- Allow asylum seekers to work, saving taxpayers' money and allowing them the dignity of earning their living instead of having to depend on handouts.

- End the detention of children in immigration detention centres.

Alternative systems such as electronic tagging, stringent reporting requirements and residence restrictions can be used for adults in families considered high flight risks.

- End deportations of refugees to countries where they face persecution, imprisonment, torture or execution and end the detention of individuals for whom removal is not possible or imminent, except where there is a significant risk of absconding.

better and more affordable homes

In a fair society, everyone should have the right to a decent home, but this is not the reality of Britain today. There should be quality social and private rented housing available for those who need or choose it. And it should be easy to keep your home warm without harming the environment; British houses are frequently poorly insulated, wasting money and contributing to global warming.

Liberal Democrats will:

- Make sure that repossession is always the last resort by changing the powers of the courts.

- Bring 250,000 empty homes back into use with cheap loans and grants as part of our job creation plan.

- Begin a national programme to insulate more homes paid for by the savings from lower energy bills.

- Make sure every new home is fully energy efficient by improving building regulations.

- Investigate reforming public sector borrowing requirements to free councils to borrow money against their assets in order to build a new generation of council homes, and allow them to keep all the revenue from these new homes. Over time, we will seek to provide a greater degree of subsidy as resources allow to increase the number of new sustainable homes being built.

- Scrap burdensome Home Information Packs, retaining the requirement for homes to have an energy performance certificate.

public transport you can rely on

Britain needs a well-run, efficient transport system. Public transport is an important part of a fair society and the best way to cut carbon emissions from transport without trying to limit people's opportunities to travel.

We want to improve the experience for the traveller and cut carbon emissions. We will:

- Switch traffic from road to rail by investing in local rail improvements, such as opening closed rail lines and adding extra tracks, paid for by cutting the major roads budget.

- Cut rail fares, changing the contracts with Train Operating Companies so that regulated fares fall behind inflation by 1 per cent each year, meaning a real-terms cut.

- Make Network Rail refund a third of your ticket price if you have to take a rail replacement bus service.

- Overhaul Network Rail to put the interests of passengers first and bring it under the Freedom of Information Act to make it more open.

- Set up a UK Infrastructure Bank to invest in public transport like high speed rail.

- Give councils greater powers to regulate bus services according to community needs so that local people get a real say over routes and fares.

- Include the promotion of safer cycling and pedestrian routes in all local transport plans.

restricting aviation growth

The emissions from rising aviation are a serious problem in the fight against climate change. But in some more remote parts of the country, flights are a vital lifeline, and aviation is important for the economy as a whole. Liberal Democrats believe that we should do all we can to ensure people use alternatives where that makes sense.

We will:

- Replace the per-passenger Air Passenger Duty with a per-plane duty (PPD), so capturing freight movements by air for the first time.

- Introduce an additional, higher rate of PPD on domestic flights for which alternative and less polluting travel is readily available.

- Cancel plans for the third runway at Heathrow and any expansion of other airports in the South East.

a fair deal for motorists

Our planned expansion of public transport will provide much-needed alternatives to private cars, and cut carbon emissions. However, in many places there will always be a need for car travel, so we need to ensure that it is as environmentally friendly as possible. We will:

- Work through the EU for a zero emissions target for all new cars by 2040 and extend targets to other vehicles.

- Undertake preparations for the introduction of a system of road pricing in a second parliament. Any such system would be revenue-neutral for motorists, with revenue from cars used to abolish Vehicle Excise Duty and reduce fuel duty, helping those in rural areas who have no alternatives to road travel. Some of the revenue from lorries would be used to fund further extensions of high speed rail through the UK Infrastructure Bank.

- Introduce a rural fuel discount scheme which would allow a reduced rate of fuel duty to be paid in remote rural areas, as is allowed under EU law.

a green and pleasant land

The beauty of Britain's natural landscape is vital to the quality of life of those who live there and to visitors. Liberal Democrats will change the way the environment is protected so everyone has fair access to clean water, clean air, and open spaces. We're the only party that takes seriously the responsibility of protecting our natural inheritance and ensuring access for all.

Liberal Democrats will:

- Increase the general right of access to the countryside, along the lines of the model introduced by the Liberal Democrats in Scotland.

- Abolish the Infrastructure Planning Commission and return decision-making, including housing targets, to local people. We will create a third-party right of appeal in cases where planning decisions go against locally agreed plans.

- Set targets for 'zero waste', aiming to end the use of landfill. That means less packaging, more recycling, and a huge increase in anaerobic digestion to generate energy from food and farm waste. We will also improve resource efficiency and reduce waste through requiring better design and durability product standards and reducing excess packaging.

- Introduce a new strategy to bring the UK back on target to halt the loss of habitats and species and as far as possible restore biodiversity by 2020.

- Protect greenfield land and our built heritage by reducing the cost of repairs. We will equalise VAT on new build and repair on an overall revenue-neutral basis. This will also help to reduce the costs of repairs to historic buildings.

- Make National Parks more democratically accountable, allowing a proportion of the Park boards to be elected.

- Create a new designation – similar to Site of Special Scientific Interest status – to protect green areas of particular importance or value to the community. We will aim to double the UK's woodland cover by 2050. We will stop 'garden grabbing' by defining gardens as greenfield sites in planning law so that they cannot so easily be built over.

manage water for everyone

Britain has real problems in managing its scarce water resources. Some people face devastating floods, while others have drought conditions most summers. We will:

- Stop major new housing developments in major flood risk areas.

- Crack down on waste from the water companies and introduce compulsory smart meters in areas of shortage.

- Introduce landscape-scale planning policies with a specific remit to restore water channels, rivers and wetlands and reduce flood risk by properly utilising the natural capacity of the landscape to retain water.

a fair deal for the countryside

Liberal Democrats are proud that we represent a large part of rural Britain. We believe a fair society is one where people can afford to work and live in the countryside with accessible public services.

Liberal Democrats will:

- Give local authorities the power to set higher Council Tax rates for second homes and the option to require specific planning permission for new second homes, in areas where the number of such homes is threatening the viability of a community.

- Through our policy on Capital Gains Tax, ensure that those who use second homes as speculative investments will pay tax on enhanced capital value at the same rate as on earned income, not at 18 per cent as at present.

- End the post office closure programme to keep post offices open in rural areas where they're the lynchpin of community life, improve access to banking and help secure the future of the Post Office through a PostBank.

- Promote schemes for affordable homes like equity mortgages and 'Home on the Farm' which encourage farmers to convert existing buildings into affordable housing.

- Refund VAT to mountain rescue services.

fair trade for British farmers

It is important to Britain's future security that the country has a sustainable farming industry. We will build on that strength and ensure that farmers get the fair deal they deserve, are able to earn a living wage and also help to protect our natural environment and heritage.

Liberal Democrats will:

- Create a legal Supermarket Code and a powerful independent regulator of Britain's food market.

- Introduce a minimum level for the Single Farm Payment and concentrate future reductions on the highest claims so that big landowners get less, and the money goes to working farmers who need it, not people who farm one field as a hobby.

- Use the money freed by our reform to Single Farm Payments to provide extra support for hill farmers, cheap loans to help farmers invest in environmentally friendly biogas digesters and a new Farming Apprenticeship scheme.

- Work within Europe for further reform of the Common Agricultural Policy, while continuing direct support for farmers, especially in upland and less favoured areas. We believe that a greater proportion of that support should be targeted at conservation, the environment and tackling climate change, as well as at providing food security for a rapidly growing world population. Organic and reduced-input foodstuffs should be encouraged.

- Help consumers to choose foods with the least environmental impact, through clearer labelling, and work with the EU to make sure country-of-origin labels identify the source of the products, not where they are packaged. We will use government procurement policy to expand the market for sustainable and fair-traded products.

supporting the voluntary sector

As Liberal Democrats, we are committed to handing power back to local communities. We believe that society is strengthened by communities coming together and engaging in voluntary activity, which sets people and neighbourhoods free to tackle local problems.

Liberal Democrats will support the voluntary sector by:

- Introducing 'easy giving accounts' at publicly-owned banks to allow people to operate charitable giving accounts alongside their current accounts.

- Reforming Gift Aid to operate at a single rate of 23 per cent – giving more money to charity while closing down a loophole for higher rate tax payers.

- Reforming the process of criminal record checking so that volunteers need only one record that is portable, rather than multiple checks for each activity.

your say. Liberal Democrats are the only party that believes in radical political reform to reinvent the way our country is run and put power back where it belongs: into the hands of people.

change that works **for you**

BUILDING A FAIRER BRITAIN

fair and local politics, protecting your freedom

Liberal Democrats are the only party which believes in radical political reform to reinvent the way our country is run and put power back where it belongs: into the hands of people. We want to see a fair and open political system, with power devolved to all the nations, communities, neighbourhoods and peoples of Britain.

As the expenses scandal showed, the political system is rotten. Hundreds of MPs have safe seats where they can ignore their constituents. Party funding rules mean big donors have huge influence. Power has been concentrated in Westminster and Whitehall by a succession of governments. And Britain's hard-won civil liberties have been eaten away.

Liberal Democrats will do things differently, because we believe that power should be in the hands of people, not politicians. We will give people a real say in who governs the country by **introducing fair votes**. We will **stop big donations** and **give people the power to sack corrupt MPs**. We will **increase the powers of the Welsh Assembly and Scottish Parliament**. We will **cut back central government and all the stifling targets** that it sets and make sure **local taxes are spent locally**. And we will introduce a **Freedom Bill** to restore the civil liberties that are so precious to the British character.

fairer politics

Liberal Democrats will transform politics. We want people to be empowered, knowing the chance to change things in their neighbourhood or in the country as a whole is in their hands.

Liberal Democrats will:

- Change politics and abolish safe seats by introducing a fair, more proportional voting system for MPs. Our preferred Single Transferable Vote system gives people the choice between candidates as well as parties. Under the new system, we will be able to reduce the number of MPs by 150.

- Give the right to vote from age 16.

- Introduce fixed-term parliaments to ensure that the Prime Minister of the day cannot change the date of an election to suit themselves.

- Strengthen the House of Commons to increase accountability. We will increase Parliamentary scrutiny of the budget and of government appointments and give Parliament control over its own agenda so that all bills leaving the Commons have been fully debated.

- Replace the House of Lords with a fully-elected second chamber with considerably fewer members than the current House.

- Get better politics for less. Liberal Democrats would save this country nearly £2 billion by reforms that cut back waste in central government and the Houses of Parliament.

- Introduce a written constitution. We would give people the power to determine this constitution in a citizens' convention, subject to final approval in a referendum.

- Strengthen the Data Protection Act and the Office of the Information Commissioner, extending Freedom of Information legislation to private companies delivering monopoly public services such as Network Rail.

cleaner politics

There has been much talk of political reform from the other two parties, but nothing has happened. They have worked together to block reform, even voting against a proposal to give people the right to sack corrupt MPs. Dependent on money from the unions and big business, they have blocked changes to party funding. And determined to protect the secrecy of the House of Commons, they had to be pushed into revealing the details of MPs' expenses in the first place. Only Liberal Democrats are able to break open this system and deliver real change.

We will:

- Give you the right to sack MPs who have broken the rules. We would introduce a recall system so that constituents could force a by-election for any MP found responsible for serious wrongdoing. We are campaigning for this right of recall to be introduced to the European Parliament too.

- Get big money out of politics by capping donations at £10,000 and limiting spending throughout the electoral cycle.

- Require all MPs, Lords and parliamentary candidates to be resident, ordinarily resident and domiciled in Britain for tax.

- Curb the improper influence of lobbyists by introducing a statutory register of lobbyists, changing the Ministerial Code so that ministers and officials are forbidden from meeting MPs on issues where the MP is paid to lobby, requiring companies to declare how much they spend on lobbying in their annual reports, and introducing a statutory register of interests for parliamentary candidates based on the current Register of Members' Interests.

more power for local people

Liberal Democrats believe local people know best about how things should be done in their area. We will radically decentralise politics so that local people have the powers and the funding to deliver what they want for their communities.

Liberal Democrats will:

- Make local government more accountable and responsive to local people by introducing fair votes for local elections in England.

- Reform local taxation. The Council Tax is an unfair tax. Liberal Democrats believe that it should be scrapped and replaced with a fair local tax, based on people's ability to pay. It is necessary to pilot Local Income Tax to resolve any practical issues of implementation before it can be rolled out nationally, so we would invite councils to put themselves forward to be involved in the piloting phase in the second year of a Parliament.

- Return business rates to councils and base them on site values, as a first step towards the radical decentralisation of taxation and spending powers to local people.

- Review local government finance completely as part of these tax changes, including reviewing the unfair Housing Revenue Account system and the mainstreaming of central grants.

- Give people a say in policing and the NHS with elected police authorities and health boards.

- Scrap nearly £1 billion of central government inspection regimes on local councils.

- Scrap the Government Offices for the Regions and regional ministers.

- Implement the Sustainable Communities Act Amendment Bill, which gives local communities the right to propose actions in their area to improve sustainability.

a federal Britain

Liberal Democrats have always led arguments for the decentralisation of political power within a federal Britain. While we welcome the progress that has been made, the job is still far from finished.

Liberal Democrats will:

- Implement the recommendations of the Calman Commission to give significant new powers and responsibilities to the Scottish Parliament.

- Give the National Assembly primary legislative powers so that it becomes a true Welsh Parliament. We also support passing on a greater number of responsibilities to the National Assembly.

- Replace the current Barnett formula for allocating funding to the Scottish, Welsh and Northern Irish governments with a new needs-based formula, to be agreed by a Finance Commission of the Nations.

- Address the status of England within a federal Britain, through the Constitutional Convention set up to draft a written constitution for the UK as a whole.

Tensions between Labour and the SNP have undermined the devolved settlement in Scotland. This has led to unjustified and unnecessary financial disputes which have locked up money due to Scotland. We will restore revenue to Scotland from the reserves of Registers of Scotland and from Scottish money paid to OFGEM under the Fossil Fuel Levy as one-off payments in the 2011 budget and give control of future revenues to the Scottish Government. This will likely lead to an increase in revenue for Scotland of around £250 million in 2011–12.

restoring your freedoms

Liberal Democrats believe it is an individual's right to live their lives as they see fit, without discrimination, with personal privacy, and with equal rights before the law.

Decades of Labour and Conservative rule have overthrown some of the basic principles of British justice and turned Britain into a surveillance state.

Liberal Democrats will protect and restore your freedoms. We will:

- Introduce a Freedom Bill. We will regulate CCTV, stop councils from spying on people, stop unfair extradition to the US, defend trial by jury, and stop children being fingerprinted at school without their parents' permission.

- Restore the right to protest by reforming the Public Order Act to safeguard non-violent protest even if it offends; and restrict the scope of injunctions issued by vested interests.

- Protect free speech, investigative journalism and academic peer-reviewed publishing through reform of the English and Welsh libel laws – including by requiring corporations to show damage and prove malice or recklessness, and by providing a robust responsible journalism defence.

- Scrap intrusive Identity Cards and have more police instead, and also scrap plans for expensive, unnecessary new passports with additional biometric data.

- Halt the increase in unnecessary new offences with the creation of a 'stop unit' in the Cabinet Office. Every department in Whitehall would have to convince this unit of the need for a new offence.

- End plans to store your email and internet records without good cause.

- Remove innocent people from the police DNA database and stop storing DNA from innocent people and children in the future, too.

- Ensure that everyone has the same protections under the law by protecting the Human Rights Act.

- Scrap the intrusive ContactPoint database which is intended to hold the details of every child in England.

We believe that the best way to combat terrorism is to prosecute terrorists, not give away hard-won British freedoms. That is why we will:

- Reach out to the communities most at risk of radicalisation to improve the relationships between them and the police and increase the flow of intelligence.

- Scrap control orders, which can use secret evidence to place people under house arrest.

- Reduce the maximum period of pre-charge detention to 14 days.

- Make it easier to prosecute and convict terrorists by allowing intercept evidence in court and by making greater use of post-charge questioning.

If we are to be able to deliver the radical changes proposed in this manifesto as well as restoring the health of the public finances, we must be honest with people about how these policies will be paid for.

credible and responsible finances

stabilising Britain's finances to deliver our promises

If we are to be able to deliver the radical changes proposed in this manifesto as well as restoring the health of the public finances, we must be honest with people about how these policies will be paid for. That is why we have set out here how our tax package will be funded, where we intend to increase spending and where we plan to make savings.

The savings we have identified far outweigh the amount of spending we are proposing, and it is these savings which will be used to start to reduce the deficit. All the savings we have identified are either instead of or additional to proposals the Government has already made. It is our working assumption that we will start to reduce the deficit from 2011–12 onwards.

The savings identified below are only the start of a programme to tackle the deficit and in government we will go further, holding a comprehensive review of all government spending, on which we will consult fully with the public. This will identify the remaining savings which will need to be made to balance the government's books. This comprehensive review will not reverse or undermine any of the spending commitments we make in this manifesto.

Over and above our planned new levy on the profits of banks, we will seek to eliminate the deficit through spending cuts. If, in order to protect fairness, sufficient cuts could not be found, tax rises would be a last resort. While it will be impossible to remove the Government's tax rises while the deficit is so huge, the increase in National Insurance Contributions is a damaging tax on jobs and an unfair tax on employees, so when resources allow we would seek to reverse it.

Following the election of a Liberal Democrat Government, an emergency budget and interim spending review would be held by no later than the end of June 2010. This budget and spending review would have four purposes:

- To put in place the necessary tax changes in order to raise the personal allowance to £10,000 for the start of the financial year 2011–12.

- To put in place cuts which could be realised within the financial year, such as scrapping the Child Trust Fund or restricting tax credits, to release money for our jobs and infrastructure package.

- Subject to our five economic tests being met, to put into place cuts for 2011–12 identified in our manifesto.

- To confirm the departmental spending shifts necessary to deliver our core manifesto commitments.

We will establish a Council on Financial Stability, involving representatives of all parties, the Governor of the Bank of England, and the Chair of the Financial Services Authority. This group would agree the timeframe and scale of a deficit reduction plan to set the framework (though not the detail) for the Comprehensive Spending Review and seek to promote it externally and domestically. Any such agreement would be without prejudice to parties retaining and advocating distinctive views on a wide range of issues, such as fair taxes and spending priorities.

Throughout the summer and early autumn a Comprehensive Spending Review of all departments would be conducted with the objective of identifying the remaining cuts needed to, at a minimum, halve the deficit by 2013–14. A Strategic Security and Defence Review would form part of this spending review, working within the same financial and time constraints.

This review will focus particularly on savings that can be made across government – such as on pay, public sector pensions, and IT provision –

and on low-priority spending. It will not reverse or undermine any of the spending commitments that we make in this manifesto.

In education, that means that additional funding for schools through the Pupil Premium will continue to be delivered throughout the next Parliament. Instead of ring-fencing education, we are doing better than that by bringing in new money to fund the Pupil Premium.

In health, our first priority will continue to be to increase spending in some parts of the NHS by cutting waste in others. We do not plan to make net cuts in spending on front-line health services.

The cross-government economies needed to reduce the deficit such as on pay, pensions, and IT procurement will affect all departments, so it would simply be dishonest to say that entire departmental budget can be ring-fenced from cuts. For example, it is only because we refuse to ring-fence departments from the search for savings that we have been able to identify the funds for the Pupil Premium and to protect frontline health services.

The results of this spending review would be widely consulted on with the public sector and general public throughout the end of 2010 and beginning of 2011. Based on this consultation a full spending review up to 2013–14 would be published alongside the 2011 Budget.

tax proposals

	£m in projected 2011–12 prices[1]
Costs of proposals	
1 Raise the personal allowance to £10,000 per person	16,795
Total	**16,795**
Revenue generated from proposals	
Closing tax loopholes and cutting reliefs that benefit the wealthiest	
2 Reform capital gains tax	1,920
3 Restrict pension tax relief to the basic rate	5,455
4 A 1 per cent levy on the value of properties over £2m	1,710
Green taxation	
5 Switching from Air Passenger Duty to a per-plane duty	3,060
6 A higher per-mile duty charge for non-lifeline domestic flights	255
Anti-avoidance measures	
7 Income tax and National Insurance Contributions	2,415
8 Corporation tax	1,460
9 Stamp duty	750
Total	**17,025**
Contingency fund	**230**

Note: tables may not sum due to rounding

[1] All figures have been rounded to the nearest £5m

spending proposals

£m (in predicted nominal terms)[1]

		2010–11	2011–12	2012–13	2013–14	2014–15
	Spending commitments					
1	Jobs and infrastructure package including:[2]					
1a	Eco cash-back scheme	335	0	0	0	0
1b	Investing in wind energy and other renewables	420	0	0	0	0
1c	Insulating public buildings	400	0	0	0	0
1d	Bringing empty homes back into use	1,165	0	0	0	0
1e	Tackling youth unemployment	660	95	0	0	0
1f	Bus scrappage scheme	140	0	0	0	0
2	Cut class sizes – introducing a pupil premium[3]	0	2,500	2,540	2,590	2,640
3	Scrapping tuition fees[3]	600	685	740	1,570	1,765
4	Restore the pension earnings link	0	0	320	325	330
5	Recruit 3,000 more police officers[4]	5	50	95	140	185
6	A pay rise and better homes for our troops	0	420	425	430	440
	Total spending	**3,730**	**3,745**	**4,115**	**5,050**	**5,360**

savings proposals

		£m (in predicted nominal terms)[1]				
		2010–11	2011–12	2012–13	2013–14	2014–15
Helping people fairly						
7	Reform tax credits	640	1,305	1,300	1,310	1,315
8	Reform winter fuel payments	300	145	60	-15	-70
9	Scale back the Homebuy programme	250	255	260	265	270
10	Refocus Train to Gain	325	335	340	345	350
11	End government contributions to the Child Trust Fund	395	545	555	565	580
12	Introduce a levy on bank profits	2,005	2,205	2,430	2,670	2,940
13	Cut Ministry of Defence administration and top brass	0	205	420	440	460
14	Cut the economic costs of mental health problems through better treatment	0	425	500	575	605
15	A cash limit on public sector pay rises of £400 for 2 years [5]	0	1,705	3,460	3,525	3,600
Decentralising government						
16	Abolish the Government Offices for the Regions	0	90	90	90	95
17	Reform Regional Development Agencies	0	600	610	620	635
18	Cut bureaucracy of local government inspection	0	860	870	890	905
19	End top-down education initiatives	0	335	340	350	355
Creating a freer society						
20	Scrap ID cards	50	80	110	155	155
21	Scrap biometric passports	220	405	425	400	380
22	Scrap Intercept Modernisation Programme	0	200	200	200	200
23	Abolish ContactPoint	0	45	45	50	50
24	Maintain the current school leaving age	0	0	35	35	70

credible and responsible finances

		2010–11	2011–12	2012–13	2013–14	2014–15
Creating a more cost-effective government						
25	Commercialise UK Trade and Investment	0	135	135	140	140
26	Scrap Eurofighter tranche 3B	0	0	510	510	510
27	Cut education quangos and administration	0	415	410	420	430
28	Prison reform	0	795	735	675	845
29	Scrap civil service bonuses	0	155	155	160	160
30	Cut use of consultants in the public sector	0	180	180	185	190
31	Cut quangos across government	0	225	225	230	235
32	Cut the costs of politics	0	610	620	635	645
Net increase in devolved administration budgets[6]						
33	The Scottish Parliament[7]	240	-120	-120	-30	-25
34	The National Assembly for Wales	140	-15	-15	30	40
35	The Northern Ireland Assembly	80	-50	-45	-15	-15
	Total savings	3,730	12,430	15,205	15,435	16,050
	Net increase in public sector spending	0	-8,680	-11,090	-10,385	-10,685

Note: Totals may not sum due to rounding

[1] All figures have been rounded to the nearest £5m

[2] The jobs package with the exception of parts 1c and 1e is for England only. Barnett consequences for the remainder are accounted for in lines 33 to 35

[3] Costs are for England, Barnett consequences for the devolved administrations are accounted for in lines 33 to 35

[4] Costs are for England and Wales only, Barnett consquences for Scotland and Northern Ireland are accounted for in lines 33 and 35

[5] This proposal is an alternative to the Government's proposal to cap public sector pay at 1%

[6] Scottish and Welsh Liberal Democrats have set out their own budget plans for Scotland and Wales

[7] As set out in this manifesto, a Liberal Democrat Government would resolve the disputes and anomalies between the UK and Scottish Governments over the Registers of Scotland and the Scottish element of the Fossil Fuel Levy, with the consequence of adding up to £250m to the resources controlled by the Scottish Government in 2011–12.

manifesto 2010 index